Anonymus

Helps to Worship

A Manual for Holy Communion and Daily Prayer

Anonymus

Helps to Worship
A Manual for Holy Communion and Daily Prayer

ISBN/EAN: 9783742837493

Manufactured in Europe, USA, Canada, Australia, Japa

Cover: Foto ©Thomas Meinert / pixelio.de

Manufactured and distributed by brebook publishing software
(www.brebook.com)

Anonymus

Helps to Worship

Helps to Worship;

𝕬 𝕸𝖆𝖓𝖚𝖆𝖑

FOR

HOLY COMMUNION

AND

DAILY PRAYER.

Compiled by Two Priests.

DEDICATED, BY PERMISSION, TO

THE LORD BISHOP OF OXFORD.

A. R. MOWBRAY & CO.;

Oxford: **London:**

116, S. ALDATE'S STREET. | WARWICK LANE. E.C.

TO

𝕿𝖍𝖊 𝕽𝖎𝖌𝖍𝖙 𝕽𝖊𝖛𝖊𝖗𝖊𝖓𝖉 𝕱𝖆𝖙𝖍𝖊𝖗 𝖎𝖓 𝕲𝖔𝖉,

JOHN FIELDER,

LORD BISHOP OF OXFORD,

THIS MANUAL,

WITH HIS LORDSHIP'S KIND PERMISSION,

IS RESPECTFULLY DEDICATED

BY

TWO OF HIS CLERGY.

RECOMMENDATORY NOTICE.

I accept the dedication of this book with much pleasure from the friends who publish it.

So far as I have examined it, I find reason to hope that it will be of real service to such as use it with attention and care.

J. F. OXON.

Preface.

THIS book contains but little original. In drawing it up from devotions already more or less in use, we have had chiefly in view the needs of the boys and young men of our own communicant classes ; but while we hope that our little work may be found useful, and not too difficult, for such as require only simple forms, it has been our endeavour, by the insertion of a certain number of alternative devotions in the part for Holy Communion, to make it also of service to those who look for something fuller and more advanced.

We have to render grateful thanks to those authors who have kindly allowed us to make use of their works, especially to the compiler of "The Guide to Heaven," and "The Way of Life," and the author of "Devotions before and after Holy Communion ;" as also to the editors of "Hymns Ancient and Modern," for the use of certain hymns, and, amongst others who have given us similar leave, to Messrs. Richardson and Sons, for the use of the late Rev. F. W. Faber's hymn "Jesu, Gentlest Saviour," and Mr. Chatterton Dix, for the hymn, "Alleluia, sing to Jesus," from his "Altar Songs."

We send out this book with the earnest desire that God may bless it to the good of those who use it, and in the hope that the compilers may not be forgotten in the prayers of those who derive from it any benefit.

C. B.
H. G. M.

Newbury, 1877.

Contents.

Morning Prayer.

Kneel down, remember that you are in God's Presence, and then say :

IN the Name of the Father, and of the Son, and of the Holy Ghost. Amen.

Lord, have mercy upon us.
Christ, have mercy upon us.
Lord, have mercy upon us.

OUR Father, which art in heaven, Hallowed be Thy Name. Thy kingdom come. Thy will be done in earth, As it is in heaven. Give us this day our daily bread. And forgive us our trespasses, As we forgive them that trespass against us. And lead us not into temptation ; But deliver us from evil : For Thine is the kingdom, The power and the glory, For ever and ever. Amen.

I HUMBLY thank Thee, O heavenly Father, for keeping me safe through the past night. I pray Thee to keep me in body and soul under Thy care during this day.

MAKE me, O God, really sorry that I so often sin against Thee, and of Thy great mercy forgive me. Keep me this day

B

from all evil thoughts, all bad words, and all wrong actions ; make me pure and truthful, honest and kind, diligent at my work, obedient to my parents and masters, and loving towards God and man ; for Jesus Christ's sake. Amen.

HAVE mercy, O most gracious God, upon all men. Bless especially my father and mother, my brothers and sisters, my relations and friends, and all whom I love or who are kind to me. Bless also the Clergy of this parish. Have pity upon the sick and and suffering. Give us food and clothing, keep us in good health, comfort us in all our troubles, make us to please Thee in all we do, and bring us safe at last to our home in heaven ; through Jesus Christ our Lord. Amen.

COME, O Holy Ghost, into my heart. Give me strength to fight this day against the evil one, and to resist my besetting sin.

GOD the Father, God the Son, and God the Holy Ghost, bless, preserve and keep us now and for evermore. Amen.

Mid-day Prayer.

If you have time, try to use the following prayers :

IN the name of the Father, and of the Son, and of the Holy Ghost. Amen.

O MOST Gracious Jesus, our Lord and our God, Who as at this hour didst bear our sins in Thine own Body on the Cross, have mercy upon us, we beseech Thee, both now and at the hour of our death. Amen.

O MY God, Who hast kept me safe from the morning until now, still keep me safe from every danger to my body. Give me pardon for the wrong I have already done, and grant that, serving Thee faithfully until the evening of this day, I may be preserved unto everlasting life; through Jesus Christ our Lord. Amen.

OUR Father, which art in heaven, Hallowed be Thy Name. Thy kingdom come. Thy will be done in earth, As it is in heaven. Give us this day our daily bread. And forgive us our trespasses, As we forgive them that trespass against us. And lead us not into temptation; But deliver us from evil: For Thine is the kingdom, The power, and the glory, For ever and ever. Amen.

GOD the Father, God the Son, God the Holy Ghost, bless, preserve, and keep us now and for evermore. Amen.

Evening Prayer.

*Kneel down, remember that you are in God's Presence,
and then say :*

IN the Name of the Father, and of the Son,
and of the Holy Ghost.   Amen.

Lord, have mercy upon us.
Christ, have mercy upon us.
Lord, have mercy upon us.

OUR Father, which art in heaven, Hallowed
be Thy Name.   Thy kingdom come.
Thy will be done in earth, As it is in heaven.
Give us this day our daily bread.   And forgive
us our trespasses, As we forgive them that
trespass against us.   And lead us not into
temptation ; But deliver us from evil : For
Thine is the kingdom, The power, and the
glory, For ever and ever.   Amen.

O HEAVENLY Father, Who hast kept me
safe through this day, I thank Thee for
this and all Thy other mercies.

Shew me, I pray Thee, by the help of Thy
Holy Spirit, how I have sinned against Thee
this day in thought, in word and in deed.

*Then try to remember your sins of the day, and ask
yourself such questions as these:*

1. What wrong thing have I done to-day ?
2. What sinful words have I used ?

3. What bad thoughts have I given way to?
4. Have I left undone anything that I ought to have done? and if so, what?
5. Have I fallen into my besetting sin? and if so, how often?

Then confess your sins in sorrow before God, and say:

I CONFESS, O God, that I have not obeyed Thee as I ought to do. Make me really sorry for my sins. Forgive me what I have done wrong to-day (*here name the sins you have found out by self-examination*), and all the sins of my past life, and help me to love Thee more, and serve Thee better for the time to come, for the sake of Jesus Christ, my Lord and Saviour. Amen.

HAVE mercy, O most gracious God, upon all men. Bless especially my father and mother, my brothers and sisters, my relations and friends, and all whom I love, or who are kind to me. Bless also the Clergy of this parish. Have pity upon the sick and suffering. Give us food and clothing, keep us in good health, comfort us in all our troubles, make us to please Thee in all we do, and bring us safe at last to our home in heaven; through Jesus Christ our Lord. Amen.

INTO Thy Hands, O Lord, I commend my spirit. May Thy holy Angels keep watch around me this night, and defend me from all evil, both in body and soul.   Amen.

GOD the Father, God the Son, and God the Holy Ghost, bless, preserve, and keep us now and for evermore.   Amen.

Occasional Prayers.

For Grace to withstand Temptation.

LORD, I beseech Thee, grant me grace to withstand the temptations of the world, the flesh, and the devil, and with pure heart and mind to follow Thee the only God; through Jesus Christ our Lord.

For the Help of the Holy Ghost.

O GOD, forasmuch as without Thee I am not able to please Thee; mercifully grant that Thy Holy Spirit may in all things direct and rule my heart; through Jesus Christ our Lord.

For Faith.

GIVE me, O Lord my God, a firm and living faith in Thee, that I may believe all that Thou teachest in the Holy Scriptures, and in Thy Holy Church, for Jesus' sake. Amen.

For Hope.

O MERCIFUL God, Who hast set before us the promise of so many good things, grant that we may hope in Thee to the end, until our hope shall be changed into sight, for Jesus' sake. Amen.

FOR LOVE.

ALMIGHTY God, Who Thyself art Love, fill me with the spirit of Thy holy love, that my heart being kindled by Thee, I may love Thee for ever and ever, and may love all men in Thee and for Thee according to Thy will, for the sake of Jesus Christ. Amen.

FOR THE FEAR OF GOD.

O MOST Mighty God, grant me, I pray Thee, Thy Holy Spirit, that I may seek Thee with my whole heart, and serve Thee with reverence and godly fear, for Jesus Christ's sake. Amen.

FOR OBEDIENCE.

O ALMIGHTY God, Who hast taught me to love, honour, and succour my father and mother, grant that, keeping this Thy command, I may never be a cause of grief, but rather of comfort and joy to them. Help me also, O Lord, to obey in all things lawful those in authority over me. Grant that I may be respectful, painstaking, and honest; not answering again, but with good will doing my work, as to the Lord, and not to men; for Jesus Christ's sake. Amen.

For Good Temper.

O LORD Jesus Christ, Who, when Thou wast reviled, reviledst not again, give me grace to follow Thy example in all meekness and patience. Keep me from sulkiness and loss of temper; and grant that, bearing no malice nor hatred in my heart, but being ready and willing to forgive, I may be forgiven by Thee, Who with the Father and the Holy Ghost livest and reignest, One God, world without end. Amen.

For Purity.

O ETERNAL God, Who art of purer eyes than to behold evil, of Thy mercy help me in temptation, and keep me from all impure thoughts, indecent words, and unholy actions. Let Thy Blessed Spirit of purity descend upon me, and preserve me chaste and spotless, clean and undefiled, that my body may be a holy temple, and my soul a dwelling-place, fit for Thee to dwell in; and grant that so living before Thee in all purity here, I may be presented to Thee hereafter washed and cleansed in the Blood of Thy Holy Lamb, Jesus Christ our Lord and Saviour. Amen.

For Honesty.

O ALMIGHTY God, Who out of Thine abundance givest to all men that which

seemeth best in Thy sight; give me grace to
keep my hands from picking and stealing, and
to be in all things honest before Thee in my
daily work and life; through Jesus Christ our
Lord. Amen.

For Truth.

O LORD God, Who knowest the very secrets of our hearts; root out of my
heart all hypocrisy and deceit, that I may be
truthful and upright in all that I do and say.
Keep me from evil speaking, lying, and slander-
ing; and help me, that, ever following after
truth, I may serve Thee in all sincerity of purpose; through Jesus Christ our Lord. Amen.

For Contentment.

O LORD Jesus Christ, Who, though Thou
wast rich, yet for our sakes didst become
poor; keep me, I beseech Thee, from all
covetous desires, and help me to be thankful
and contented in that state of life unto which
I am called by Thee, to Whom with the Father
and the Holy Spirit be all glory for evermore.
Amen.

For Humility.

A LMIGHTY God, Who resistest the proud,
but givest grace to the humble; grant
that I may never be lifted up by pride, nor

exalt myself above others; but serving Thee with a meek and humble heart, may always use Thy gifts to Thy honour and glory; through Jesus Christ our Lord. Amen.

For Temperance.

O BOUNTIFUL and Gracious God, Who givest us all things richly to enjoy, suffer me not by my folly to turn Thy bounty into sin; but give me the spirit of temperance and soberness, and keep me from all excess both in eating and drinking; through Jesus Christ our Lord. Amen.

For Gentleness.

O ETERNAL God, Who dost bid us love one another, and our neighbours as ourselves; grant that I may not give way to envy or jealousy at the success of others, but that rejoicing with them in all the joys which Thou givest them, and caring for them in all their troubles, I may follow Thee Who art the true and perfect Love; through Jesus Christ our Lord. Amen.

For Perseverance.

O GOD, Who hast taught us that they only who endure to the end shall be saved; guide me in my difficulties, and strengthen me in my weakness. Let no threatenings or flatteries ever draw me from obedience to Thee; but grant that, being steadfast and unmoveable, always abounding in the work of the Lord, I may come at last to Thine unspeakable glory, through Jesus Christ our Lord. Amen.

Prayers for Others.

For the Church.

O ALMIGHTY God, preserve Thy Church from all dangers ; purify it from all corruptions, and heal its divisions, that all Christians may live together at peace with one another, and in the fear and love of Thee. Bless the Missions . of Thy Church ; and have mercy upon all the heathen, Jews, Turks, infidels and heretics, and so fetch them home, Blessed Lord, to Thy flock, that they may be made one fold under one Shepherd, Jesus Christ our Lord. Amen.

For the Clergy.

B LESS, we beseech Thee, O Lord, the Bishops and Clergy of Thy Church, especially the Bishop of this Diocese, and the Clergy of this Parish, that they may handle Thy holy things with holiness, and be pleasing to Thee, Who art our Priest for ever, Jesus Christ our Lord. Amen.

For those in Authority.

H AVE mercy, O God, upon our Queen, and all that are in authority under her, or who bear rule over us. Give them an earnest

C

care for their own souls, and for the welfare of
those who are in any way committed to their
charge. Grant them prudence and wisdom, and
to us Thy people give the spirit of obedience
and love, for the sake of our Lord and Saviour
Jesus Christ. Amen.

For our Home.

VISIT, we beseech Thee, O Lord, our home
and family, and drive far from it all the
snares of the enemy. Let Thy holy angels dwell
herein to preserve us in peace, and let Thy
blessing be upon us evermore ; through Jesus
Christ our Lord. Amen.

For Friends.

STRETCH forth, O Lord, Thy mercy over all
my dear friends (especially * ————),
and bless them exceeding abundantly above all
that I can ask or think. Help us in this world
to love each other in Thee and for Thee, and in
the world to come unite us for ever at Thy feet,
where peace and love are perfect and immortal,
and Thou, with the Father and the Holy Ghost,
livest and reignest ever One God, world without
end. Amen.

* Here name any one for whom you wish specially
to pray.

For Enemies.

O LORD Jesus Christ, Who didst pray for those who crucified Thee, forgive, I pray Thee, all who have vexed me, or have behaved unkindly to me, and all, if any, who are my enemies. Do Thou forgive them, and make me forgive them from my heart, even as I look for forgiveness from Thee. Amen.

For the Sick and Suffering.

LOOK down in pity, O merciful Lord, upon all who are in trouble or suffering, either of mind or body (especially ————). Teach them that Thy hand is laid upon them in mercy and love, and help them to turn to Thee. Give them patience under their sufferings, and in Thine own good time deliver them from all their afflictions, for the sake of Jesus Christ our Lord. Amen.

For the Tempted.

O LORD Jesus Christ, Who for our sakes wast tempted by Satan in the wilderness, we pray Thee to help all Thy servants, who are now sore tried by any special temptation. Make them to stand fast in Thee ; and as Thou knowest their several weaknesses, let each one find Thee mighty to save, to Whom with the Father and the Holy Ghost be all glory for ever. Amen.

For Sinners.

ALMIGHTY God, I beseech Thee to hear my prayers for all who sin against Thee, or neglect to serve Thee, and grant unto them true repentance and an earnest longing for Thy service ; through Jesus Christ our Lord.   Amen.

For those about to be Confirmed.

ALMIGHTY and Everlasting God, I beseech Thee to bless all those who are now preparing for Confirmation.   Grant that they may approach that Holy Rite with bodies undefiled, watchful minds, and pure hearts, that so, being blessed by Thy servant the Bishop, and strengthened by Thy Good Spirit, they may never be ashamed to confess the faith of Christ Crucified, but manfully to fight under His banner against sin, the world, and the devil, and continue His faithful soldiers and servants unto their lives' end ; through Jesus Christ our Lord. Amen.

Various Prayers.

GRACE BEFORE MEALS.

BLESS, O Lord, these Thy gifts to our use, and ourselves to Thy service ; for Jesus Christ's sake. Amen.

GRACE AFTER MEALS.

FOR these and all His mercies, God's holy Name be blest and praised. Amen.

BEFORE SERVICE.

O LORD, I am now in Thy Presence ; help me by Thy Holy Spirit, that I may be ready to offer the sacrifice of praise, and to hear Thy Holy Word. Guard my mind from wandering thoughts, and my body from irreverent actions, and make my service acceptable unto Thee, through Jesus Christ our Lord. Amen.

AFTER SERVICE.

O LORD, I thank Thee that I have been in Thy Presence to glorify and praise Thee. Whatsoever in this Thy service I have done amiss, in thought word, or deed, through the weakness of the flesh, the perversity of the will, or the malice of the devil, do Thou, O most merciful Father, graciously pardon for the sake of Thy Son, Jesus Christ our Lord. Amen.

Preparation for Holy Communion.

A Prayer to be used every day in the week before you receive the Holy Communion.

O BLESSED Lord Jesus Christ, Who dost bid even me, unworthy, to come unto Thee in the Blessed Sacrament of Thy Body and Blood, prepare my soul and my body, I pray Thee, to receive Thee. Give me true sorrow for my past sins, faith in Thee Who didst die upon the Cross to save me, firm purpose to keep from all that displeases Thee, and charity to forgive all who may have vexed me. Lord, come to me that Thou mayest cleanse me. Lord, come to me that Thou mayest heal me. Lord, come to me that Thou mayest strengthen me. And grant that having received Thee, I may not forget Thee, or drive Thee from me, by being careless about pleasing Thee, but may continue Thine for ever. Amen.

On Friday, or some other day before your Communion, ask yourself very carefully the following questions, first saying:

O GOD of Truth, make me, I pray Thee, to know myself. Pour Thy light into the dark places of my heart, that I may see my grievous sins, and tell them truly unto Thee.

And this I ask through Jesus Christ our Lord.
Amen.

Since my last Communion :

1. Have I fallen into any special sin, which
is troubling my mind, and keeping me back
from God ?

2. Have I honestly tried to love and serve
God ?

3. Have I said my prayers reverently and
carefully every night and morning ?

4. Have I sworn or used bad words?

5. Have I laughed and joked, or listened to
others doing so, about religion and holy things ?

6. Have I been to Church every Sunday, and
kept the rest of the day as I ought ?

7. When I have been to Church, have I been
attentive and reverent, kneeling down, &c. ?

8. Have I been honest and diligent in my
work, or have I been slothful and idle, and
wasted my master's or employer's time?

9. Have I been obedient at home, and to
those set over me ?

10. Have I been patient under reproof, not
answering again, &c. ?

11. Have I quarrelled with anyone, or lost
my temper? thought or spoken evil of another,
been unkind, or sulky ?

12. If I have quarrelled with anyone, have
I tried to make it up ?

13. Have I been envious of others ? or proud
or conceited about myself ?

14. Have I done anything impure, or said anything impure, or encouraged any impure thought?

15. Have I taken more than I ought to eat, or to drink?

16. Have I been dishonest, or stolen anything?

17. Have I told a lie? or deceived anyone in word or act?

18. Have I grumbled at my lot, or been discontented, or covetous?

19. Have I in any way helped or encouraged others in what is wrong?

20. Have I been regular in my times of receiving the Holy Communion?

21. Was I careful about my preparation and thanksgiving at my last Communion? and have I tried to keep the resolutions I then made?

Then kneel down and confess your sins to God very humbly, saying,

I CONFESS to Thee, O God, that I have sinned through my fault, through my own great fault, by . . . . . (*here name the sins you have found out by self-examination.*) O Lord, give me true sorrow; forgive me these, and all my many sins which I have forgotten. O let me not fall from Thee any more. Hear me, and have mercy upon me, for Jesus Christ's sake, my Lord and Saviour. Amen.

N.B.—If you have any trouble in your mind, or cannot quiet your own conscience, either from some sin that you have committed, or from doubts as to whether you ought to come to Holy Communion, do not be afraid to go to your Clergyman, and ask him to help you. Mark well these words at the end of the first Exhortation in the Communion Office, Book of Common Prayer.

" And because it is requisite that no man should come to the Holy Communion, but with a full trust in God's mercy, and with a quiet conscience : therefore if there be any of you, who by this means cannot quiet his own conscience herein, but requireth further comfort or counsel, let him come to me, or to some other discreet and learned Minister of God's Word, and open his grief ; that by the ministry of God's Holy Word he may receive the benefit of absolution, together with ghostly counsel and advice, to the quieting of his conscience, and avoiding of all scruple and doubtfulness."

Also on Saturday night or Sunday morning use the following Office of Preparation :—

REMEMBER not, Lord, our offences, nor the offences of our forefathers, neither take Thou vengeance of our sins.

> Lord, have mercy upon us.
> Christ, have mercy upon us.
> Lord, have mercy upon us.

OUR Father, which art in heaven, Hallowed be Thy Name. Thy kingdom come. Thy will be done in earth, As it is in heaven. Give us this day our daily bread. And forgive us our trespasses, As we forgive them that trespass against us. And lead us not into temptation ; But deliver us from evil. Amen.

Lord, have mercy upon me : heal my soul, for I have sinned against Thee.

Cleanse Thou me from my secret faults : and keep Thy servant from presumptuous sins.

O Lord, hear my prayer, and let my cry come unto Thee.

O LORD, we beseech Thee, visit and cleanse our consciences, that when Thy Son our Lord Jesus Christ cometh, He may find in us a dwelling place prepared for Himself, through the same Jesus Christ our Lord. Amen.

I DESIRE, O gracious Lord, from this moment to renounce everything that may displease Thee, and resolve, through the grace of Thy holy Sacrament, to resist all temptations, and to become wholly Thine ; for in my own strength I can do nothing ; but on Thee I depend entirely, O my Saviour and best Friend. For Thy Name's sake, O Lord, for Thy love's sake, for Thy promise's sake, teach me whatever Thou wouldst have me to do, and then help me to do it. Teach me first what to resolve upon, and then enable me to perform my resolutions, that I may walk with Thee in the ways of holiness here, and rest with Thee in happiness hereafter.   Amen.

O Jesu, Bread of Life, lo ! my soul waiteth for Thee, send me not away fasting, lest I faint by the way.

·O Jesu, Fountain of Life, my soul thirsteth after Thee ; O let me draw water with joy out of the wells of salvation.

O Jesu, Beloved, fairer than the sons of men, draw me after Thee with the cords of Thy love.

O Jesu, jealous for souls, Whose delight is to be with the sons of men, may I love Thee, and all in and for Thee.   Amen.

GOD the Father, God the Son, God the Holy Ghost, be with me, and with mine, now and at the hour of death.   Amen.

THE DAY OF COMMUNION.

Be careful to be at Church in good time, and while waiting for the Service to begin, say one or more of these prayers :

ALMIGHTY, Everlasting God, behold I draw near to the Sacrament of the Body and Blood of Thy Son our Lord Jesus Christ ; come sick to the Physician of life, unclean to the Fountain of mercy, blind to the Light of

eternal brightness, poor and needy to the Lord
of all things ; I pray Thee, therefore, to wash
my defilements, to enlighten my blindness, to
enrich my poverty, to clothe my nakedness ;
that I may receive the true Bread of Angels, the
King of kings, and Lord of lords, with a humble,
lowly, and contrite heart, with a lively faith in
Thy mercy, and a pure desire to do Thy will.
Grant this, O God, I beseech Thee, for the sake
of the same, Thy Son our Lord Jesus Christ.
Amen.

O MOST loving Father, grant unto me that
as I desire here to receive Thy Blessed
Son veiled from sight under the form of bread
and wine, so I may hereafter behold Him face
to face, where with Thee, O Father, and the
Holy Ghost, He liveth and reigneth, ever One
God, world without end.   Amen.

B LESS, O Lord, Thy Priest, who is now
about to offer before Thee this holy
Sacrifice, as a memorial of the One Sacrifice of
Thy Dear Son upon the Cross.   I desire to join
in offering It as an act of homage and worship :
in remembrance of His Death and Passion : in
thanksgiving for all Thy blessings to Thy whole
Church, and especially for those given to me
a sinner : in prayer for the pardon of all my ·
sins, and of those of all others : and to obtain
grace and blessing for myself and for all who
are near or dear to me, and for Thy whole

Church. Hear us, O God, and accept and bless this our Service, for His sake Whose Death we are now about to commemorate : Jesus Christ our Lord. Amen.

If you have any more time before the Service begins, you can use Psalms 43, 84, or 130, in your Prayer Books.

THE ORDER

OF THE ADMINISTRATION OF

THE HOLY COMMUNION.

THE LORD'S PRAYER.

OUR Father, Which art in Heaven, Hallowed be Thy Name : Thy Kingdom come : Thy Will be done in earth, As it is in Heaven : Give us this day our daily bread : And forgive us our trespasses, As we forgive them that trespass against us : And lead us not into temptation : But deliver us from evil. Amen.

THE COLLECT FOR PURITY.

ALMIGHTY God, unto Whom all hearts be open, all desires known, and from Whom no secrets are hid : cleanse the thoughts of our hearts by the inspiration of Thy Holy Spirit, that we may perfectly love Thee, and worthily magnify Thy holy Name ; through Christ our Lord. *Amen.*

THE TEN COMMANDMENTS.

Minister.

GOD spake these words and said : I am the Lord thy God : thou shalt have none other gods but Me.

People. Lord, have mercy upon us, and incline our hearts to keep this law.

Minister. Thou shalt not make to thyself any graven image, nor the likeness of any thing that is in heaven above, or in the earth beneath, or in the water under the earth. Thou shalt not bow down to them, nor worship them : for I the Lord thy God am a jealous God, and visit the sins of the fathers upon the children unto the third and fourth generation of them that hate Me, and shew mercy unto thousands in them that love Me, and keep My commandments.

People. Lord, have mercy upon us, and incline our hearts to keep this law.

Minister. Thou shalt not take the Name of the Lord thy God in vain : for the Lord will not hold him guiltless, that taketh His Name in vain.

People. Lord, have mercy upon us, and incline our hearts to keep this law.

Minister. Remember that thou keep holy the Sabbath-day. Six days shalt thou labour and do all that thou hast to do ; but the seventh day is the Sabbath of the Lord thy God. In it thou shalt do no manner of work, thou, and thy son, and thy daughter, thy man-servant, and thy maid-servant, thy cattle, and the stranger that is within thy gates. For in six days the Lord made heaven and earth, the sea, and all that in them is, and rested the seventh day : wherefore the Lord blessed the seventh day and hallowed it.

People. Lord, have mercy upon us, and incline our hearts to keep this law.

Minister. Honour thy father and thy mother ; that thy days may be long in the land which the Lord thy God giveth thee.

People. Lord, have mercy upon us, and incline our hearts to keep this law.

Minister. Thou shalt do no murder.

People. Lord, have mercy upon us, and incline our hearts to keep this law.

Minister. Thou shalt not commit adultery.

People. Lord, have mercy upon us, and incline our hearts to keep this law.

Minister. Thou shalt not steal.

People. Lord, have mercy upon us, and incline our hearts to keep this law.

Minister. Thou shalt not bear false witness against thy neighbour.

People. Lord, have mercy upon us, and incline our hearts to keep this law.

Minister. Thou shalt not covet thy neighbour's house, thou shalt not covet thy neighbour's wife, nor his servant, nor his maid, nor his ox, nor his ass, nor anything that is his.

People. Lord, have mercy upon us, and write all these Thy laws in our hearts, we beseech Thee.

THE· COLLECT FOR THE QUEEN.

Let us pray.

A LMIGHTY God, Whose Kingdom is ever lasting, and power infinite ; have mercy upon the whole Church ; and so rule the heart of Thy chosen Servant *Victoria*, our Queen and Governour, that she, knowing Whose Minister she is, may above all things seek Thy honour and glory ; and that we and all her subjects, duly considering Whose authority she hath, may faithfully serve, honour, and humbly obey her, in Thee, and for Thee, according to Thy blessed Word and ordinance ; through Jesus Christ our Lord, Who with Thee and the Holy Ghost, liveth and reigneth, ever One God, world without end. *Amen.*

Or,

A LMIGHTY and Everlasting God, we are taught by Thy holy Word, that the hearts of Kings are in Thy rule and governance, and that Thou dost dispose and turn them as it seemeth best to Thy godly wisdom ; we humbly beseech Thee so to dispose and govern the heart of *Victoria*, Thy Servant, our Queen and Governour, that in all her thoughts, words, and works she may ever seek Thy honour and glory, and study to preserve Thy people committed to her charge in wealth, peace, and godliness : Grant this, O merciful Father, for Thy dear Son's sake, Jesus Christ our Lord. *Amen.*

Then follows the Collect for the Day, which you will find in your Prayer Book.

THE EPISTLE.

THE HOLY GOSPEL.

Before which you may say, Glory be to Thee, O Lord, *and afterwards,* Praise be to Thee, O Christ.

THE CREED.

I BELIEVE in One God, the Father Almighty, Maker of heaven and earth, and of all things visible and invisible :

And in One Lord Jesus Christ, the Only-Begotten Son of God ; Begotten of His Father before all worlds ; God of God, Light of Light, Very God of Very God, Begotten, not made ; Being of one Substance with the Father; By Whom all things were made ; Who for us men, and for our salvation, came down from heaven, AND WAS INCARNATE BY THE HOLY GHOST OF THE VIRGIN MARY, AND WAS MADE MAN ; And was crucified also for us under Pontius Pilate : He suffered and was buried ; And the third day He rose again according to the Scriptures ; And ascended into heaven, And sitteth on the right hand of the Father. And He shall come again with glory, to judge both the quick and the dead : Whose kingdom shall have no end.

And I believe in the Holy Ghost, The Lord and Giver of life; Who proceedeth from the Father and the Son ; Who, with the Father and the Son together, is worshipped and glorified ; Who spake by the Prophets. And I believe one Catholick, and Apostolick Church. I acknowledge one Baptism for the remission of sins ; And I look for the Resurrection of the dead, And the life of the world to come. Amen.

Then the alms are collected, while the Priest says one or more of the following Sentences. Always give something if you can, but do not think that you need stay away from Holy Communion if you have nothing to give. When you have made your offering, kneel down, and say :—

Blessed be Thou, Lord God of Israel, our Father, for ever and ever. All that is in the heaven and in the earth is Thine. All things come of Thee, and of Thine Own have we given Thee. Graciously accept, O Lord, these our offerings from Thine unworthy servants, for Jesus Christ's sake. Amen.

THE OFFERTORY SENTENCES.

LET your light so shine before men, that they may see your good works, and glorify your Father which is in Heaven.—*St. Matt.* v.

Lay not up for yourselves treasure upon the

earth; where the rust and moth doth corrupt, and where thieves break through and steal: but lay up for yourselves treasures in Heaven; where neither rust nor moth doth corrupt, and where thieves do not break through and steal.—*St. Matt.* vi.

Whatsoever ye would that men should do unto you, even só do unto them; for this is the Law and the Prophets.—*St. Matt.* vii.

Not every one that saith unto me, Lord, Lord, shall enter into the Kingdom of Heaven; but he that doeth the will of my Father which is in Heaven.—*St. Matt.* vii.

Zacchæus stood forth, and said unto the Lord, Behold, Lord, the half of my goods I give to the poor; and if I have done any wrong to any man, I restore fourfold.—*St. Luke* xix.

Who goeth a warfare at any time of his own cost? Who planteth a vineyard, and eateth not of the fruit thereof? Or who feedeth a flock, and eateth not of the milk of the flock?— 1 *Cor.* ix.

If we have sown unto you spiritual things, is it a great matter if we shall reap your worldly things?—1 *Cor.* ix.

Do ye not know, that they who minister about holy things live of the sacrifice; and they who wait at the Altar are partakers with the Altar? Even so hath the Lord also ordained, that they who preach the Gospel should live of the Gospel.—1 *Cor.* ix.

He that soweth little shall reap little ; and he that soweth plenteously shall reap plenteously. Let every man do according as he is disposed in his heart, not grudgingly, or of necessity ; for God loveth a cheerful giver.—*2 Cor.* ix.

Let him that is taught in the Word minister unto him that teacheth, in all good things. Be not deceived, God is not mocked : for whatsoever a man soweth that shall he reap.—*Gal.* vi.

While we have time, let us do good unto all men ; and specially unto them that are of the household of faith.—*Gal.* vi.

Godliness is great riches, if a man be content with that he hath : for we brought nothing into the world, neither may we carry any thing out. —1 *Tim.* vi.

Charge them who are rich in this world, that they be ready to give, and glad to distribute ; laying up in store for themselves a good foundation against the time to come, that they may attain eternal life.—1 *Tim.* vi.

God is not unrighteous, that He will forget your works, and labour that proceedeth of love ; which love ye have shewed for His Name's sake, who have ministered unto the Saints, and yet do minister.—*Heb.* vi.

To do good, and to distribute, forget not ; for with such sacrifices God is well pleased.— *Heb.* xiii.

Whoso hath this world's good, and seeth his brother have need, and shutteth up his com-

passion from him, how dwelleth the love of
God in him?—1 *St. John* iii.

Give alms of thy goods, and never turn thy
face from any poor man; and then the face of
the Lord shall not be turned away from thee.—
Tobit iv.

Be merciful after thy power. If thou hast
much give plenteously : if thou hast little, do
thy diligence gladly to give of that little : for
so gatherest thou thyself a good reward in the
day of necessity.—*Tobit* iv.

He that hath pity upon the poor lendeth unto
the Lord : and look, what he layeth out, it shall
be paid him again.—*Proverbs* xix.

Blessed be the man that provideth for the
sick and needy : the Lord shall deliver him in
the time of trouble.—*Psalm* xli.

*The Priest now puts the Bread and Wine on the Altar.
While this is being done, use the following Prayer :—*

Mindful of Thy precepts, O Lord, we offer to
Thee these our Oblations of Bread and Wine :
grant that the fulness of Thy Blessing may rest
upon them, and that through the Power of the
Holy Ghost, we may indeed receive the Body
and Blood of Jesus Christ our Saviour. Amen.

THE PRAYER FOR THE CHURCH.

Let us pray for the whole state of Christ's
Church militant here in earth.

ALMIGHTY and everliving God, Who by
Thy holy Apostle hast taught us to make

prayers and supplications, and to give thanks, for all men ; .

We humbly beseech Thee most mercifully to accept our Alms and Oblations, and to receive these our prayers, which we offer unto Thy Divine Majesty;

Beseeching Thee to inspire continually the Universal Church with the spirit of truth, unity, and concord: And grant, that all they that do confess Thy Holy Name may agree in the truth of Thy Holy Word, and live in unity and godly love.

We beseech Thee also to save and defend all Christian Kings, Princes, and Governors ; and specially Thy Servant Victoria our Queen ; that under her we may be godly and quietly governed: And grant unto her whole Council, and to all that are put in authority under her that they may truly and indifferently minister justice, to the punishment of wickedness and vice, and to the maintenance of Thy true religion, and virtue.

Give grace, O Heavenly Father, to all Bishops and Curates, *(especially the Bishop of this Diocese, and the Clergy of this parish,)* that they may both by their life and doctrine set forth Thy true and lively Word, and rightly and duly administer Thy Holy Sacraments ;

And to all Thy people give Thy heavenly grace *(especially* ———,*)* and especially to this congregation here present, that with meek heart and due reverence, they may hear, and receive Thy Holy Word ; truly serving Thee in holiness and righteousness all the days of their life.

And we most humbly beseech Thee of Thy goodness, O Lord, to comfort and succour all them, who in this transitory life, are in trouble, sorrow, need, sickness, or any other adversity (*especially* ————).

And we also bless Thy Holy Name for all Thy Servants departed this life in Thy faith and fear (*especially* ————) ; beseeching Thee to give us grace, so to follow their good examples, that, with them, we may be partakers of Thy Heavenly Kingdom :

Grant this, O Father, for Jesus Christ's sake, our only Mediator and Advocate. *Amen.*

THE EXHORTATION.

(*This is not always used.*)

D EARLY beloved in the Lord, ye that mind to come to the Holy Communion of the Body and Blood of our Saviour Christ, must consider how Saint Paul exhorteth all persons diligently to try and examine themselves, before they presume to eat of that Bread, and drink of that Cup. For as the benefit is great, if with a true penitent heart and lively faith we receive that holy Sacrament ; for then we spiritually eat the Flesh of Christ, and drink His Blood ; then we dwell in Christ, and Christ in us ; we are one with Christ, and Christ with us; so is the danger great, if we receive the same unworthily. For then we are guilty of the Body and Blood of Christ our Saviour; we eat and drink our own damnation, not considering the Lord's Body; we kindle God's wrath against us; we provoke Him to plague us with divers diseases, and sundry kinds of death. Judge therefore yourselves, brethren, that ye be not judged of the Lord; repent you truly for your sins past; have a lively and steadfast faith in Christ our Saviour; amend your lives, and be in perfect charity with all men; so shall ye be meet partakers of those Holy Mysteries. And above all things ye must give most humble and hearty thanks to God, the Father, the Son, and the Holy Ghost, for the redemption of the world by the Death and Passion of our Saviour Christ, both God and Man; Who did humble Himself, even to the death upon the Cross, for us, miserable sinners, who lay in darkness and the shadow of death; that He might make us the children of God, and exalt us to everlasting life. And to the end that we should alway remember the exceeding great love of our Master, and Only Saviour, Jesus Christ, thus dying for us, and the innumerable benefits which by His precious blood-shedding He hath obtained to us; He hath instituted and ordained Holy Mysteries, as pledges of His love, and for a continual remembrance of His death, to our great and endless comfort.

To Him therefore, with the Father and the Holy Ghost, let us give, as we are most bounden, continual thanks ; submitting ourselves wholly to His holy will and pleasure, and studying to serve Him in true holiness and righteousness all the days of our life. *Amen.*

THE INVITATION.

YE that do truly and earnestly repent you of your sins, and are in love and charity with your neighbours, and intend to lead a new life, following the commandments of God, and walking from henceforth in His holy ways; Draw near with faith, and take this holy Sacrament to your comfort ; and make your humble confession to Almighty God, meekly kneeling upon your knees.

THE GENERAL CONFESSION.

Say this after the Minister.

ALMIGHTY God, Father of our Lord Jesus Christ, Maker of all things, Judge of all men ; We acknowledge and bewail our manifold sins and wickedness, Which we, from time to time, most grievously have committed, By thought, word, and deed, Against Thy Divine Majesty, Provoking most justly Thy wrath and indignation against us. We do earnestly repent, And are heartily sorry for these our misdoings ; The remembrance of them is grievous unto us : The burden of them is intolerable. Have mercy

upon us, Have mercy upon us, most merciful
Father ; For Thy Son, our Lord Jesus Christ's
sake, Forgive us all that is past ; And grant
that we may ever hereafter Serve and please
Thee In newness of life, To the honour and
glory of Thy Name ; Through Jesus Christ our
Lord. Amen.

The Absolution.

ALMIGHTY God, our Heavenly Father,
Who of His great mercy hath promised
forgiveness of sins, to all them that with hearty
repentance and true faith turn unto Him ; have
mercy upon you ; pardon and deliver you from
all your sins ; confirm and strengthen you in all
goodness ; and bring you to everlasting life ;
through Jesus Christ our Lord. *Amen.*

The Comfortable Words.

HEAR what comfortable words our Saviour
Christ saith unto all that truly turn to
Him.

Come unto Me all that travail and are heavy
laden, and I will refresh you.—*S. Matt.* xi. 28.

So God loved the world, that He gave His
Only-Begotten Son, to the end that all that
believe in Him should not perish, but have everlasting life.—*S. John* iii. 16.

Hear also what Saint Paul saith.

This is a true saying, and worthy of all men

to be received : that Christ Jesus came into the world to save sinners.—1 *Tim.* i. 15.

Hear also what Saint John saith.

If any man sin, we have an Advocate with the Father, Jesus Christ the Righteous ; and He is the Propitiation for our sins.—1 *S. John* ii. 2.

Then shall the Priest say,

Lift up your hearts.

Answer. We lift them up unto the Lord.
Priest. Let us give thanks unto our Lord God.
Answer. It is meet and right so to do.

THE PREFACE.

IT is very meet, right, and our bounden duty, that we should at all times, and in all places, give thanks unto Thee, O Lord, Holy Father, Almighty, Everlasting God.

Here on certain days is said the Proper Preface, printed below, or else immediately follows :

THEREFORE with Angels and Archangels, and with all the Company of Heaven, we laud and magnify Thy glorious Name; evermore praising Thee, and saying,

THE SANCTUS.

Say this after the Priest.

HOLY, Holy, Holy, Lord God of Hosts, Heaven and earth are full of Thy glory : Glory be to Thee, O Lord most High. Amen.

PROPER PREFACES.

Upon Christmas Day, *and seven days after.*

BECAUSE Thou didst give Jesus Christ Thine Only Son to be born as at this time for us ; Who by the operation of the Holy Ghost, was made Very Man of the substance of the Virgin Mary His Mother : and that without spot of sin, to make us clean from all sin. Therefore with Angels, &c.

Upon Easter Day, *and seven days after.*

BUT chiefly are we bound to praise Thee for the glorious Resurrection of Thy Son Jesus Christ our Lord : for He is the very Paschal Lamb, Which was offered for us, and hath taken away the sin of the world : Who by His Death hath destroyed death, and by His Rising to life again hath restored to us everlasting life. Therefore with Angels, &c.

Upon Ascension Day, *and seven days after.*

THROUGH Thy most dearly Beloved Son Jesus Christ our Lord ; Who after His most glorious Resurrection manifestly appeared to all His Apostles, and in their sight ascended up into Heaven to prepare a place for us ; that where He is, thither we might also ascend, and reign with Him in glory. Therefore with Angels, &c.

Upon Whitsun Day, *and six days after.*

THROUGH Jesus Christ our Lord, according to Whose most true promise, the Holy Ghost came down as at this time from Heaven with a sudden great sound, as it had been a mighty wind, in the likeness of fiery tongues, lighting upon the Apostles, to teach them and to lead them to all truth ; giving them both the gift of divers languages, and also boldness with fervent zeal constantly to preach the Gospel unto all nations ; whereby we have been brought out of darkness and error into the clear light and true knowledge of Thee, and of Thy Son Jesus Christ.   Therefore with Angels, &c.

Upon the Feast of Trinity *only.*

WHO art One God, One Lord ; not One only Person, but Three Persons in One Substance.   For that which we believe of the glory of the Father, the same we believe of the Son, and of the Holy Ghost, without any difference or inequality.   Therefore with Angels, &c.

THE PRAYER OF HUMBLE ACCESS.

WE do not presume to come to this Thy Table, O Merciful Lord, trusting in our own righteousness, but in Thy manifold and great mercies.   We are not worthy so much as to gather up the crumbs under Thy Table.   But Thou art the same Lord, Whose property is always to have mercy : Grant us therefore, Gracious Lord, so to eat the Flesh of Thy dear Son Jesus Christ, and to drink His Blood, that our sinful bodies may be made clean by His Body, and our souls washed through His most precious Blood, and that we may evermore dwell in Him, and He in us. *Amen.*

While the Priest is preparing to consecrate, say this Prayer,

Have mercy upon us, O Lord our God, after Thy great mercy, and send down upon these gifts lying now before Thee, Thy Holy Ghost, that He may make this bread the Holy Body, and this cup the Blood of Thy Christ; that They may be to us who partake of Them for the remission of sins, and for the sanctification of soul and body unto life everlasting. Amen.

Blessed is He that cometh in the Name of the Lord, Hosanna in the Highest.

THE PRAYER OF CONSECRATION.

ALMIGHTY God, our Heavenly Father, Who of Thy tender mercy didst give Thine only Son Jesus Christ to suffer death upon the Cross for our redemption ; Who made there (by His one Oblation of Himself once offered,) a full, perfect, and sufficient Sacrifice, Oblation, and Satisfaction, for the sins of the whole world : and did institute, and in His Holy Gospel command us to continue, a perpetual memory of that His precious Death until His coming again ;

Hear us, O merciful Father, we most humbly beseech Thee ; and grant that we receiving these Thy creatures of Bread and Wine, according to Thy Son our Saviour Jesus Christ's holy institution, in remembrance of His Death and Passion, may be partakers of His most blessed Body and Blood :

Who in the same night that He was betrayed, *took Bread ; and, when He had given thanks, †He brake it, and gave it to His disciples, saying, Take, eat ; ‡THIS IS MY BODY, WHICH IS GIVEN FOR YOU: do this in remembrance of Me.

* Here the Priest is to take the Paten into his hands :

† And here to break the Bread :

‡ And here to lay his hand upon all the Bread.

Likewise after supper, §He took the Cup ; and when He had given thanks, He gave it to them, saying, Drink ye all of this ; for THIS‖ IS MY BLOOD OF THE NEW TESTAMENT, WHICH IS SHED FOR YOU AND FOR MANY FOR THE REMISSION OF SINS ; Do this, as oft as ye shall drink It, in remembrance of Me. *Amen.*

§ Here he is to take the Cup into his hand.

‖ And here to lay his hand upon every vessel (be it chalice or flagon) in which there is any wine to be consecrated.

DEVOTIONS AFTER THE PRAYER OF CONSECRATION.

During the pause while the Priest is communicating, worship and adore your Lord now very near to you in His Holy Sacrament.

ACTS OF ADORATION.

I.

O Lamb of God, That takest away the sins of the world; Have mercy upon us.

O Lamb of God, That takest away the sins of the world; Have mercy upon us.

O Lamb of God, That takest away the sins of the world; Grant us Thy peace.

II.

Thee we adore, O hidden Saviour, Thee,
Who in Thy Sacrament dost deign to be;
Both flesh and spirit at Thy Presence fail,
Yet here Thy Presence we devoutly hail.

O blest Memorial of our dying Lord,
Who living Bread to men doth here afford!
O may our souls for ever feed on Thee,
And Thou, O Christ, for ever precious be.

Fountain of goodness, Jesu, Lord and God,
Cleanse us, unclean, with Thy most cleansing
Blood;

Increase our faith and love, that we may know
The hope and peace which from Thy Presence
   flow.

O Christ, Whom now beneath a veil we see,
May what we thirst for soon our portion be,
To gaze on Thee unveiled, and see Thy Face,
The vision of Thy glory and Thy grace. Amen.

III.

I worship and adore Thee, O Lord Jesus
Christ, present in Thy Holy Sacrament. I
worship Thee, O Blessed Saviour, Prince of
Peace! the Virgin's Holy Son! Hope of sinners!
King of Saints! Joy of Angels! Perfect God
and Perfect Man! I adore Thee, O my Lord,
my God. I believe in Thee; Lord, I believe,
help Thou mine unbelief. I praise Thee, I
thank Thee, for all Thy great love to me. O
that I might love Thee as I ought, O Lord, my
Helper, my Redeemer. Thou, O Lord God,
art the thing that I long for; Thou art my
Hope, even from my youth. O be Thou my
only Joy, my fulness of Delight, the Strength of
my heart, and my Portion for ever. Amen.

INTERCESSIONS AND PRAYERS.

I.

And now, O Father, mindful of the love
   That bought us, once for all, on Calvary's
      Tree,

And having with us Him that pleads above,
  We here present, we here spread forth to Thee
That only Offering perfect in Thine eyes,
The one true, pure, immortal Sacrifice.

Look, Father, look on His anointed Face,
  And only look on us as found in Him ;
Look not on our misusings of Thy grace,
  Our prayer so languid, and our faith so dim ;
For lo ! between our sins and their reward
We set the Passion of Thy Son our Lord.

And then for those, our dearest and our best,
  By this prevailing Presence we appeal ;
O fold them closer to Thy mercy's breast,
  O do Thine utmost for their souls' true weal ;
From tainting mischief keep them white and
    clear,
And crown Thy gifts with strength to persevere.

And so we come ; O draw us to Thy feet,
  Most patient Saviour, Who canst love us still ;
And by this Food, so awful and so sweet,
  Deliver us from every touch of ill ;
In Thine own service make us glad and free,
And grant us never more to part with Thee.
                    Amen.

II.

O ALMIGHTY Father, we Thine unworthy
servants, having in remembrance Thy
Dear Son, our Lord Jesus Christ, His blessed

Passion, and precious Death, His mighty Resurrection, and glorious Ascension : and rendering unto Thee most hearty thanks for the innumerable benefits procured unto us by the same, do now celebrate and make here before Thy Divine Majesty the Memorial He hath commanded us to make, as we offer unto Thee these Thy Gifts, even the Holy Bread of eternal life, and the Cup of everlasting salvation ;

Looking upon which with favourable countenance, mercifully accept, we beseech Thee, this our offering, and grant that all we, who shall be partakers of this Holy Communion, may so worthily receive the most precious Body and Blood of Thy Son, Jesus Christ, that He may evermore dwell in us, and we in Him.

Remember also, O Lord, Thy servants and handmaids, (especially . . . .) who have gone before us in Thy faith and fear; and to all these who rest in Christ, grant, we beseech Thee, refreshment, light, and peace.

And to us sinners, Thy servants, who trust in the multitude of Thy mercies, and to all others for whom we ought to pray (especially . . . .) vouchsafe to grant some portion and fellowship with Thy Holy Saints and Martyrs, into whose company we beseech Thee to admit us, not weighing our merits, but pardoning our offences through the same Jesus Christ our Lord, by Whom and with Whom, in the Unity of the Holy Ghost, all honour and glory be unto

Thee, O Father Almighty, world without end. Amen.

*If you have time for any other Prayers before Communi-
cating, you can use some of those on pp. 7—16; or else
some of the Hymns at the end of this Book : but immediately before going up to the Altar, say : —*

O BLESSED Jesus, the God of my heart, and the Life of my soul; as the hart panteth after the waterbrooks, so doth my soul pant after Thee, the Fountain of life. O come, blessed Jesu, and take full possession of my heart for ever. I offer it unto Thee without re-serve, I desire to consecrate it eternally to Thee; I believe in Thee; I hope in Thee; I love Thee above all things—at least, I desire so to love Thee : I grieve for love of Thee, that I ever offended Thee. Pardon, forgive, atone, by Thine own Self. Amen.

O Lamb of God, That takest away the sins of the world, let Thy humility and patience be offered in satisfaction for my sins. Amen.

O Lamb of God, plead before Thy Father the bitterness of Thy Passion, for my reconciliation to God. Amen.

O Lord, I am not worthy to receive Thee, but by the bitterness of Thy Passion forgive me all my sins. Amen.

O Lord, I am not worthy to receive Thee, but of Thy great mercy coming to me now in this Thy Blessed Sacrament, abide with me and leave me not for evermore. Amen.

At the Altar.

Lord, I am not worthy that Thou shouldest come under my roof.

After receiving the Sacrament of our Lord's Body.

In life, in death, O Lord, abide with me.

Before receiving the Sacrament of our Lord's Blood.

I will receive the Cup of Salvation and call upon the Name of the Lord.

Before you leave the Altar.

Jesu, my Lord, I Thee adore,
O make me love Thee more and more.

On kneeling again in your place in the Church, thank God, and use some of the following Devotions.

I.

I am my Beloved's, and my Beloved is mine. Thanks be to God for His unspeakable Gift.

Glory be to Thee, O Christ, Who hast vouchsafed to come into my unworthy soul. Give me, I pray Thee what most I need, keep me ever Thine, and let not me, who have now re- · ceived this most Holy Sacrament, fall back again into sin. Amen.

May the Soul of Christ sanctify me,
And the Body of Christ save me,
And the Blood of Christ sustain me,
And the Water from the Side of Christ wash
　　me,

And the Passion of Christ comfort me.
O good Jesu, hear me,
Within Thy wounds hide me,
Suffer me not to be separated from Thee,
From the malicious enemy defend me,
In the hour of my death call me, and bid me
come to Thee, that with all Thy Saints I may
praise Thee for ever and ever.   Amen.

II.

Jesu, gentlest Saviour
    God of Might and Power,
Thou Thyself art dwelling
    In us at this hour.

Nature cannot hold Thee,
    Heaven is all too strait,
For Thine endless Glory,
    And Thy Royal State.

Out beyond the shining
    Of the farthest star,
Thou art ever stretching
    Infinitely far.

Yet the hearts of children
    Hold what worlds cannot,
And the God of Wonders
    Loves the lowly spot.

Jesu, gentlest Saviour,
    Thou art in us now ;
Fill us full of goodness,
    Till our hearts o'erflow.

Pray the prayer within us,
  That to heaven shall rise ;
Sing the song that Angels
  Sing above the skies.

Multiply our Graces,
  Chiefly Love and Fear,
And, dear Lord, the chiefest,
  Grace to persevere.

Oh, how can we thank Thee
  For a Gift like this,
Gift that truly maketh
  Heaven's eternal bliss ?

Ah, when wilt Thou always
  Make our hearts Thine home ?
We must wait for heaven,
  Then the day will come.

Now at least we'll keep Thee
  All the time we may ;
But Thy Grace and Blessing
  We will keep alway.   Amen.

III.

O MOST Gracious and Eternal God, I bless
    and glorify Thy Holy Name, and adore
Thy Goodness, for that Thou hast once more
given me the opportunity of receiving this Thy
wondrous favour, even the Body and Blood of
my dearest Saviour.   What shall I render unto
Thee, O Lord, for all that Thou hast done unto

me ? Bless thou the Lord, O my soul, and forget not all His benefits. Thou art my God,
and I will thank Thee ; Thou art my God, and
I will praise Thee. O keep me ever in Thy
love ; take from me all affection to sin or vanity,
and grant that, seeking more and more the
things which are above, I may find in Thee
alone my Peace and Joy ; for Thy mercy's sake,
to Whom with the Son and the Holy Spirit, be
all honour and gloiy, now and for evermore.
Amen.

IV.

O LORD Jesus Christ, Who hast been
pleased to give us that greatest Gift of
Thy most holy Body, and Thy most precious
Blood, that Thou mightest join us to Thyself ;
bless me, I pray Thee, and all who have this
day received Thee. Grant that we may not
grieve Thee by any wrong thought, word or
deed, but do Thou keep our souls pure and holy
Who hast come to dwell in them : Who ever
livest and reignest with the Father and the
Holy Ghost, One God, world without end.
Amen.

V.

BEHOLD, O Lord, I have Thee now, Who
hast all things : I possess Thee, Who
possessest all things, and canst do all things :
therefore, O my God and my All, do Thou

wean my heart from all other things beside Thee, for in them there is nothing but vanity and vexation of spirit; on Thee alone may my heart be fixed; in Thee be my rest, for in Thee is my treasure, in Thee is the sovereign Truth, and true Happiness, and eternal Life.

Let my soul, O Lord, feel the sweetness of Thy Presence, may it taste how sweet Thou art. O Lord, that attracted by love of Thee, it may seek for nothing wherein to rejoice out of Thee: for Thou art the Joy of my heart, and my God, and my Portion for ever.

Thou art the Good Shepherd Who hast laid down Thy life for Thy sheep. Behold, I am that sheep which was lost, and yet Thou dost vouchsafe to feed me with Thy Body and Blood; lay me now upon Thy shoulders. What wilt Thou refuse me, Who hast given Thyself unto me? Oh! be Thou my Shepherd, and I shall lack nothing in the green pasture wherein Thou feedest me, until I am brought to the pastures of eternal life.

O King of Heaven and earth, rich in pity! Behold, I am poor and needy; Thou knowest what I most require; Thou alone art able to enrich and help me; help me, O God, and out of the treasure of Thy Goodness, succour Thou my needy soul.

O my Lord and my God! Behold, I am Thy

servant : give me understanding, and kindle my affection that I may know and do Thy will.

Thou art the Lamb of God, the Lamb without spot, Who takest away the sins of the world; take away from me whatever hurteth me and displeaseth Thee; and give me what Thou knowest to be pleasing to Thee and good for me.

If you need any further Devotions Psalms 23, 103, 150, or the Te Deum and the Magnificat, in the Prayer Book, or some of the Prayers (pp. 7—16) and Hymns (pp. 62—74) in this Book will be useful.
When all have communicated, the Priest and People together say :

THE LORD'S PRAYER.

OUR Father, Which art in Heaven, Hallowed be Thy Name : Thy Kingdom come : Thy Will be done in earth, as it is in Heaven : Give us this day our daily bread : and forgive us our trespasses, as we forgive them that trespass against us : and lead us not into temptation : But deliver us from evil : For Thine is the Kingdom, the Power, and the Glory, for ever and ever. Amen.

THE PRAYER OF OBLATION.

O LORD and Heavenly Father, we Thy humble servants entirely desire Thy Fatherly goodness mercifully to accept this our Sacrifice of Praise and Thanksgiving;

Most humbly beseeching Thee to grant, that by the Merits and Death of Thy Son Jesus Christ, and through faith in His Blood, we and all Thy whole Church may obtain remission of our sins, and all other benefits of His Passion.

And here we offer and present unto Thee, O Lord, ourselves, our souls and bodies, to be a reasonable, holy and lively sacrifice unto Thee; humbly beseeching Thee, that all we, who are partakers of this Holy Communion, may be fulfilled with Thy grace and heavenly benediction.

And although we be unworthy, through our manifold sins, to offer unto Thee any sacrifice, yet we beseech Thee to accept this our bounden duty and service; not weighing our merits, but pardoning our offences; through Jesus Christ our Lord;

By Whom and with Whom, in the Unity of the Holy Ghost, all honour and glory be unto Thee, O Father Almighty, world without end. *Amen.*

Or this:

THE THANKSGIVING.

OLMIGHTY and Everlasting God, we most heartily thank Thee, for that Thou dost vouchsafe to feed us, who have duly received these holy Mysteries, with the spiritual Food of the most precious Body and Blood of Thy Son our Saviour Jesus Christ; and dost assure us thereby of Thy favour and goodness towards us; and that we are very members incorporate in the mystical Body of Thy Son, Which is the blessed company of all faithful people; and are also heirs through hope of Thy everlasting Kingdom, by the merits of the most precious Death and Passion of Thy dear Son. And we most humbly beseech Thee, O Heavenly Father, so to assist us with Thy grace, that we may continue in that holy fellowship, and do all such good works as Thou hast prepared for us to walk in; through Jesus Christ our Lord, to Whom, with Thee and the Holy Ghost, be all honour and glory, world without end. *Amen.*

THE GLORIA IN EXCELSIS.

GLORY be to God on high, and in earth peace, good will towards men. We praise Thee, we bless Thee, we worship Thee, we glorify Thee, we give thanks to Thee for Thy great glory, O Lord God, Heavenly King, God the Father Almighty.

O Lord, the only-Begotten Son Jesu Christ; O Lord God, Lamb of God, Son of the Father, that takest away the sins of the world, have mercy upon us. Thou that takest away the sins of the world, have mercy upon us. Thou that takest away the sins of the world, receive our prayer. Thou that sittest at the right hand of God the Father, have mercy upon us.

For Thou only art Holy; Thou only art the Lord; Thou only, O Christ, with the Holy Ghost, art most High in the glory of God the Father. *Amen.*

THE BLESSING.

THE Peace of God, which passeth all understanding, keep your hearts and minds in the knowledge and love of God, and of His Son Jesus Christ our Lord :

And the Blessing of God Almighty, the Father, the Son, and the Holy Ghost, be amongst you and remain with you always. *Amen.*

PRAYER AFTER THE SERVICE.

O MOST merciful God, Who hast admitted me into Thy Presence to glorify and praise Thee, forgive all that Thou hast seen wrong or imperfect in this my service, and accept and bless the same for Jesus Christ's sake.   Amen.

Before you leave the Church, or at your prayers in the evening, you can use the following Office:—

Thanksgiving after Communion.

LORD, now lettest Thou Thy servant depart in peace : according to Thy Word.
For mine eyes have seen : Thy Salvation.
Which Thou hast prepared before the face of all people ;

To be a Light to lighten the Gentiles: and to be the Glory of Thy people Israel.

Glory be to the Father, and to the Son: and to the Holy Ghost;

As it was in the beginning, is now, and ever shall be : world without end.   Amen.

Lord, have mercy upon us.
 Christ, have mercy upon us.
Lord have mercy upon us.

OUR Father, which art in Heaven, Hallowed be Thy Name.   Thy Kingdom come. Thy Will be done in earth, As it is in Heaven. Give us this day our daily bread.   And forgive us our trespasses, As we forgive them that trespass against us.   And lead us not into temptation ; But deliver us from evil : For Thine is the Kingdom, The Power and the Glory, For ever and ever.   *Amen.*

Thou feddest Thine own people with Angels' Food, and didst give them Bread from Heaven.

Let all Thy works praise Thee, O Lord : and Thy saints give thanks unto Thee.

Not unto us, O Lord : not unto us, but to Thy Name give the glory.

O Lord, hear our prayer ; and let our cry come unto Thee.

Purify our hearts we beseech Thee, O Lord, with the fire of Thy Holy Spirit, that we may serve

Thee with a chaste body and please Thee with a pure mind.   Amen.

I RENDER Thee thanks, O Lord, Holy Father, Almighty and everlasting God, Who hast vouchsafed not for any goodness of mine, but only out of the greatness of Thy mercy, to feed me, a sinner, Thy unworthy servant, with the precious Body and Blood of Thy Son our Lord Jesus Christ ; and I pray Thee that this Holy Communion may not bring fresh guilt upon me, but may help forward the peace and salvation of my soul.   O Lord, I pray Thee by this Sacrament to strengthen my faith, to rid me of my sins, to root out my evil desires, and to make me loving, patient, and humble.   Defend me against the attacks of the Devil, and the wrong suggestions of my own heart.   Help me in true peace of soul to cling to Thee, my Lord and God, Who hast made me for Thyself.   And of Thy mercy vouchsafe to bring me at the last to Thy most holy Feast above, where Thou, with Thy Son and the Holy Ghost art to Thy Saints true Light, everlasting Joy, and perfect Happiness : through the same our Lord Jesus Christ. Amen.

I BESEECH Thee, O Lord Jesu Christ, that Thy Passion may be unto me virtue, whereby I may be preserved and defended.   Let the sprinkling of Thy Blood be to me the washing away of all my sins. Let Thy Death be to me everlasting glory, both now and ever. Amen.

THE grace of our Lord Jesus Christ, and the love of God, and the fellowship of the Holy Ghost be with us all evermore. Amen.

In addition to using the above Thanksgiving, " I render Thee thanks " *on the Day of your Communion, it would be well to repeat it at your Evening Prayers for two or three days afterwards.*

Hymns.

I.

MORNING.

NEW every morning is the love
    Our wakening and uprising prove;
Through sleep and darkness safely brought,
Restored to life, and power, and thought.

New mercies, each returning day,
Hover around us while we pray;
New perils past, new sins forgiven,
New thoughts of God, new hopes of heaven.

If on our daily course our mind
Be set to hallow all we find,
New treasures still, of countless price,
God will provide for sacrifice.

The trivial round, the common task,
Will furnish all we need to ask,
Room to deny ourselves, a road
To bring us daily nearer God.

Only, O Lord, in Thy dear love,
Fit us for perfect rest above;
And help us, this and every day,
To live more nearly as we pray.   Amen.

II.

NOW that the daylight fills the sky,
  We lift our hearts to God on high,
That He, in all we do or say,
Would keep us free from harm to-day.

May He restrain our tongues from strife,
And shield from anger's din our life,
And guard with watchful care our eyes
From earth's absorbing vanities.

O may our inward hearts be pure,
From faults of folly kept secure,
And pride of sinful flesh subdued,
Through sparing use of daily food.

So we, when this day's work is o'er,
And shades of night return once more,
Our path of trial safely trod,
Shall give the glory to our God.

All praise to God the Father be,
All praise, Eternal Son, to Thee,
Whom with the Spirit we adore
For ever and for evermore.   Amen.

III.

EVENING.

THE day is past and over :
  All thanks, O Lord, to Thee,
I pray Thee now that sinless
  The hours of dark may be :
O Jesu, keep me in Thy sight,
And guard me through the coming night.

The joys of day are over ;
　I lift my heart to Thee,
And ask Thee that offenceless
　The hours of dark may be :
O Jesu, keep me in Thy sight,
And guard me through the coming night.

The toils of day are over ;
　I raise the hymn to Thee,
And ask that free from peril
　The hours of dark may be :
O Jesu, keep me in Thy sight,
And guard me through the coming night.

Be Thou my soul's preserver,
　For Thou alone dost know
How many are the perils
　Through which I have to go :
O loving Jesu, hear my call,
And guard and save me from them all. Amen.

IV.

SUN of my soul, Thou Saviour dear ;
　　It is not night if Thou be near :
O may no earth-born cloud arise
To hide Thee from Thy servant's eyes.

When the soft dews of kindly sleep
My wearied eyelids gently steep,
Be my last thought, how sweet to rest
For ever on my Saviour's breast.

Abide with me from morn till eve,
For without Thee I cannot live :
Abide with me when night is nigh,
For without Thee I dare not die.

If some poor wandering child of Thine
Have spurned to-day the voice Divine,
Now, Lord, the gracious work begin ;
Let him no more lie down in sin.

Watch by the sick ; enrich the poor
With blessings from Thy boundless store ;
Be every mourner's sleep to-night,
Like infant's slumbers, pure and light.

Come near and bless us when we wake,
Ere through the world our way we take ;
Till in the ocean of Thy love
We lose ourselves in heaven above. Amen.

V.

THE HOLY COMMUNION.

NOW, my tongue, the mystery telling
  Of the glorious Body sing,
And the Blood, all price excelling,
  Which the Gentiles' Lord and King,
In a Virgin's womb once dwelling,
  Shed for this world's ransoming.

Word-made-Flesh true bread He maketh
  By His Word His Flesh to be ;
Wine His Blood ; which whoso taketh
  Must from carnal thoughts be free ;
Faith alone, though sight forsaketh,
  Shews true hearts the mystery.

Therefore we, before Him bending,
  This great Sacrament revere ;
Types and shadows have their ending,
  For the newer rite is here ;
Faith, our outward sense befriending,
  Makes our inward vision clear.

Glory let us give, and blessing
  To the Father, and the Son,
Honour, might, and praise addressing,
  While eternal ages run ;
Ever too His love confessing,
  Who from Both with Both is **One.** **Amen.**

VI.

ONCE, only once, and once for all,
    His precious life He gave ;
Before the Cross our spirits fall,
  And own it strong to save.

"One offering, single and complete,"
  With lips and heart we say :
But what He never can repeat
  He shews forth day by day.

For, as the Priest of Aaron's line
  Within the Holiest stood,
And sprinkled all the mercy-shrine
  With sacrificial blood ;

So He, Who once atonement wrought
  Our Priest of endless power,
Presents Himself for those He bought
  In that dark noontide hour.

His manhood pleads where now It lives
  On heaven's eternal Throne,
And where in mystic rite He gives
  Its Presence to His own.

And so we shew Thy death, O Lord,
  Till Thou again appear ;
And feel, when we approach Thy Board,
  We have an Altar here.

All glory to the Father be,
  All glory to the Son,
All glory, Holy Ghost, to Thee,
  While endless ages run.   Amen.

VII.

BEFORE COMMUNION.

LO ! the Angels' Food is given
    To the pilgrim who hath striven ;
See the children's Bread from heaven,
    Which on dogs may ne'er be spent :
Truth the ancient types fulfilling
Isaac bound, a victim willing,
Paschal Lamb its life-blood spilling,
    Manna to the fathers sent.

Very Bread, Good Shepherd, tend us ;
Jesu, of Thy love befriend us ;
Thou refresh us, Thou defend us,
Thine eternal goodness send us
    In the land of life to see :
Thou Who all things canst and knowest,

Who on earth such Food bestowest,
Grant us with Thy Saints, though lowest,
Where the heavenly Feast Thou showest,
    Fellow heirs and guests to be.   Amen.

VIII.

O FOOD that weary pilgrims love,
    O Bread of Angel-hosts above,
    O Manna of the Saints,
The hungry soul would feed on Thee ;

O Fount of love, O cleansing Tide,
Which from the Saviour's piercèd Side
    And Sacred Heart dost flow,
Be ours to drink of Thy pure rill,
Which only can our spirits fill,
    And all our need bestow.

Lord Jesu, Whom, by power Divine
Now hidden 'neath the outward sign,
    We worship and adore,
Grant, when the veil away is rolled,
With open face we may behold
    Thyself for evermore.   Amen.

IX.

ROCK of ages, cleft for me,
    Let me hide myself in Thee,
Let the Water and the Blood
From Thy riven Side which flowed,
Be of sin the double cure,
Cleanse me from its guilt and power.

Not the labours of my hands
Can fulfil Thy law's demands ;
Could my zeal no respite know,
Could my tears for ever flow,
All for sin could not atone ;
Thou must save, and Thou alone.

Nothing in my hand I bring.
Simply to Thy Cross I Cling ;
Naked, come to Thee for dress ;
Helpless, look to Thee for grace ;
Foul, I to the Fountain fly ;
Wash me, Saviour, or I die.

While I draw this fleeting breath,
When my eyelids close in death,

When I soar through tracts unknown,
See Thee on Thy Judgment Throne ;
Rock of ages, cleft for me,
Let me hide myself in Thee. Amen.

X.

JESU, Lover of my soul,
  Let me to Thy Bosom fly,
While the gathering waters roll,
  While the tempest still is high :
Hide me, O my Saviour, hide,
  Till the storm of life be past ;
Safe into the haven guide,
  O receive my soul at last.

Other refuge have I none ;
  Hangs my helpless soul on Thee ;
Leave, ah ! leave me not alone,
  Still support and comfort me.
All my trust on Thee is stayed,
  All my help from Thee I bring ;
Cover my defenceless head
  With the shadow of Thy wing.

Plenteous grace with Thee is found,
  Grace to cleanse from every sin ;
Let the healing streams abound ;
  Make and keep me pure within ;
Thou of Life the Fountain art ;
  Freely let me take of Thee ;
Spring Thou up within my heart,
  Rise to all eternity. Amen.

XI.

THANKSGIVING.

Alleluia ! His the triumph,
 His the victory alone ;
Hark ! the songs of peaceful Sion
 Thunder like a mighty flood ;
Jesus out of every nation
 Hath redeemed us by His Blood.

Alleluia ! not as orphans
 Are we left in sorrow now ;
Alleluia ! He is near us,
 Faith believes, nor questions how :
Though the cloud from sight received Him,
 When the forty days were o'er,
Shall our hearts forget His promise,
 " I am with you evermore ?"

Alleluia ! Bread of Angels,
 Thou on earth our Food, our Stay ;
Alleluia ! here the sinful
 Flee to Thee from day to day !
Intercessor, Friend of sinners,
 Earth's Redeemer, plead for me,
Where the songs of all the sinless
 Sweep across the crystal sea.

Alleluia ! King Eternal,
 Thee the Lord of lords we own ;
Alleluia ! born of Mary,
 Earth Thy footstool, heaven Thy Throne :
Thou within the veil hast entered,
 Robed in flesh, our great High Priest ;
Thou on earth both Priest and Victim
 In the Eucharistic Feast.

Alleluia ! sing to Jesus !
 His the sceptre, His the Throne ;
Alleluia ! His the triumph,
 His the victory alone ;

Hark ! the songs of peaceful Sion
 Thunder like a mighty flood ;
Jesus out of every nation
 Hath redeemed us by His Blood.   Amen.

XII.

THE King of love my Shepherd is,
 Whose goodness faileth never ;
I nothing lack if I am His
And He is mine for ever.

Where streams of living water flow
 My ransomed soul He leadeth,
And, where the verdant pastures grow,
 With food celestial feedeth.

Perverse and foolish oft I strayed,
 But yet in love He sought me,
And on His Shoulder gently laid,
 And home, rejoicing, brought me.

In death's dark vale I fear no ill
 With Thee, dear Lord, beside me ;
Thy rod and staff my comfort still,
 Thy Cross before to guide me.

Thou spread'st a Table in my sight ;
 Thy Unction grace bestoweth :
And oh, what transport of delight
 From Thy pure Chalice floweth !

And so through all the length of days
 Thy goodness faileth never :
Good Shepherd, may I sing Thy praise
 Within Thy House for ever.   Amen.

XIII.

PRAISE, my soul, the King of heaven,
  To His feet thy tribute bring;
Ransomed, healed, restored, forgiven,
  Evermore His praises sing;
    Alleluia! Alleluia!
  Praise the everlasting King.

Praise Him for His grace and favour
  To our fathers in distress;
Praise Him still the same as ever,
  Slow to chide, and swift to bless;
    Alleluia! Alleluia!
  Glorious in His faithfulness.

Father-like, He tends and spares us,
  Well our feeble frame He knows;
In His hands He gently bears us,
  Rescues us from all our foes;
    Alleluia! Alleluia!
  Widely yet His mercy flows.

Angels in the height, adore Him;
  Ye behold Him face to face;
Saints triumphant, bow before Him,
  Gathered in from every race;
    Alleluia! Alleluia!
  Praise with us the God of grace.   Amen.

XIV.

PERSEVERANCE.

SAVIOUR, blessèd Saviour,
  Listen whilst we sing;
Hearts and voices raising
  Praises to our King.

All we have we offer,
   All we hope to be,—
Body, soul, and spirit,—
   All we yield to Thee.

Farther, ever farther
   From Thy wounded side,
Heedlessly we wandered,
   Wandered far and wide ;
Till Thou cam'st in mercy
   Seeking young and old,
Lovingly to bear them,
   Saviour, to Thy fold.

Nearer, ever nearer,
   Christ, we draw to Thee,
Deep in adoration
   Bending low the knee.
Thou, for our redemption,
   Cam'st on earth to die ;
Thou, that we might follow,
   Hast gone up on high.

Great, and ever greater,
   Are Thy mercies here ;
True and everlasting
   Are the glories there ;
Where no pain or sorrow,
   Toil or care is known ;
Where the angel-legions
   Circle round Thy throne.

Dark, and ever darker,
   Was the wintry past ;
Now a ray of gladness
   O'er our path is cast ;
Every day that passeth,
   Every hour that flies,
Tells of love unfeignèd,
   Love that never dies.

D

Clearer still, and clearer,
  Dawns the light from heaven,
In our sadness bringing
  News of sins forgiven ;
Life has lost its shadows,
  Pure the light within ;
Thou hast shed Thy Radiance
  On a world of sin.

Brighter still, and brighter,
  Glows the western sun,
Shedding all its gladness
  O'er our work that's done ;
Time will soon be over,
  Toil and sorrow past,
May we, blessèd Saviour,
  Find a rest at last !

Onward, ever onward,
  Journeying o'er the road
Worn by Saints before us,
  Journeying on to God ;
Leaving all behind us,
  May we hasten on,
Backward never looking
  Till the prize is won.

Higher then, and higher,
  Bear the ransomed soul,
Earthly toils forgotten,
  Saviour, to its goal ;
Where, in joys unthought of,
  Saints with angels sing,
Never weary, raising
  Praises to their King.   Amen.

A. R. Mowbray & Co., Printers, Oxford.

www.ingramcontent.com/pod-product-compliance
Lightning Source LLC
Chambersburg PA
CBHW031454270326
41930CB00007B/988